SOME ENGLISH QUICK TIPS

30+ Ways for Older Teens and Young Adults to Correct Most Common Errors in Writing, Grammar and Spelling

ISRAELIN SHOCKNESS
Successful Youth Living - Vol. 5

Copyright © 2021 by Israelin Shockness.

Requests for information can be obtained by contacting info@IsraelinShockness.com.

Cataloguing-in-Publication Data
Israelin Shockness
Includes bibliographical references
ENGLISH QUICK TIPS
30+ Ways for Older Teens and Young Adults to Correct Everyday Errors in Writing, Grammar and Spelling
ISBN: 978-1-7750094-2-9 (ebook)
ISBN: 978-1-7750094-7-4 (paperback)
SERIES – Successful Youth Living - Vol. 5

All rights reserved. No part of this publication may be reproduced, stored in a retrieval system, or transmitted in any form or by any means electronic, mechanical, photocopy, recording, or any other except for brief quotations in printed reviews, without the prior permission of the author (info@IsraelinShockness.com).

DISCLAIMER

The materials provided in this book are intended to provide quick answers to basic grammatical, writing and spelling questions that often occur in writing English. The various concepts that are covered in these materials are intended to help the reader identify some of the common errors that often appear in written work. This is not a complete book on English grammar. Exercises are intended to reinforce what was presented and vocabularies are intended to expand on the reader's own vocabulary. The opinions expressed in this book are solely those of this author and not those of the publisher. Further, the publisher is exempt from any responsibility for actions taken by readers with respect to the content. The publisher also acknowledges that readers act of their own accord in using information presented and hold the author and the publisher blameless in the readers' use of the content.

PURPOSE OF THIS SERIES

Successful Youth Living is a series of books, dealing with issues, which older teens and young adults face as they go through the uncertainty of adolescence. A few of the topics dealt with are: becoming a leader in your own right without being a bully; learning how to assume responsibility; fostering positive attitudes and habits for self-growth; learning how to continue your education regardless of where you stopped or whether you dropped out; developing emotional intelligence and caring for self and others; learning how to deal with stress; recognizing the importance of personal reflection; and being a person that others admire for the right reasons.

The 'seed' for these volumes was actually planted when the author, then a teenager on a scholarship, almost dropped out of university because of her inability to deal with many issues that had nothing to do with school.

Thanks to the insightfulness and mentorship of a professor, the author became a teen mentor and since then have committed herself to paying it forward by looking out for vulnerable teens and young adults that have lost their way, the way she had almost lost hers. After years of further study, a career as an educator working with children, teens and young adults, years as a volunteer in marginalized communities and as a columnist in a weekly community newspaper, Israelin has recognized that many of the issues plaguing adolescents have not changed. She has therefore decided to share ideas she has gleaned from personal experience, as well as from her students, readers, studies, and from peer-reviewed articles.

DEDICATION

This book is dedicated to all my teachers who insisted over the years that anything worth doing was worth doing well and who took pains to ensure that I learned to pay attention to what I sometimes thought were only small details that did not really matter.

I also dedicate this book to all the young people who may often ignore the details of writing and who have developed their own shortcuts to communication. Although this practice of using shortcuts may work in the informal world of friends and acquaintances, it often leaves the formal world of academia and employers at a loss. Take the time to give some attention to the basic rules of written English.

WHY THIS BOOK?

Yet, it is embarrassing to find grammatical errors in writing on billboards, in promotional letters, and even in news reports. The effects of this failing are that important messages are often not given the attention they deserve, as some readers may dismiss the sender of the messages as less than expert, and this could very well sabotage a first impression. Finding grammatical errors in cover letters accompanying resumes could also make the difference between taking an applicant seriously and deciding to hire him or her or rejecting his or her application as inadequate.

This book is provided for all those who may want or need to improve their English grammar, punctuation, writing, and comprehension, or who may be interested in giving some attention to grammatical correctness. **Some English Quick Tips** is by no means a complete work on English grammar, but it may prove useful as a refresher for those who have been out of school for a while, who may have forgotten, or who may still be working on learning some basic grammatical rules. This book may also provide some help for expanding vocabulary and improving punctuation and spelling.

Being able to write correctly without help can prove useful. This book therefore addresses some of the common errors in basic English writing that are often overlooked. These are also some of the basic errors that are flagged on admission tests and letters for colleges and universities, as well as on Human Resources assessment tests for certain jobs.

"Learning is a treasure that will follow its owner everywhere." **- Chinese Proverb**

Recommendation

We recommend, as you go through this book, that you actually make notes and complete the exercises given. By writing down notes and completing exercises, you will be reinforcing what you have read. This will quite likely help you in the future to spot errors in your writing. If you are a kinesthetic learner, the act of writing things down rather than typing them will very likely help you to remember them better.

Get a special notebook for this purpose. Make this even more interesting by working along with a friend or classmate.

Confucius is quoted as saying: *"I hear and I forget. I see and I remember. I do and I understand."* Take this counsel and do the exercises.

Successful Youth Living – Vol. 5

SOME ENGLISH QUICK TIPS – 30+ Ways for Older Teens and Young Adults to *Correct Most Common Errors in Writing, Grammar and Spelling*

TABLE OF CONTENTS

CHAPTER 1: PARTS OF SPEECH 15

CHAPTER 2: WHAT IS A NOUN? 19

CHAPTER 3: NOUNS - SINGULAR AND PLURAL 23

CHAPTER 4: UNUSUAL PLURALS 29

CHAPTER 5: NOUNS SHOWING POSSESSION 35

CHAPTER 6: DO NOT FORM PLURALS USING THE APOSTROPHE 37

CHAPTER 7: VERBS 39

CHAPTER 8: TYPES OF VERBS (Continued) 43

CHAPTER 9: TYPES OF VERBS (Continued) 45

CHAPTER 10: TENSES AND VERB FORMS 47

CHAPTER 11: FORMING TENSES 53

CHAPTER 12: SOME PROBLEM VERBS 57

CHAPTER 13: MORE PROBLEM VERBS 59

CHAPTER 14: MORE PROBLEM VERBS 61

CHAPTER 15: MORE PROBLEM VERBS 63

CHAPTER 16: OTHER FORMS OF VERBS – VERBALS 67

CHAPTER 17: INFINITIVE OF PURPOSE 71

CHAPTER 18: PRONOUNS 73

CHAPTER 19: PRONOUN-ANTECEDENT AGREEMENT 77

CHAPTER 20: ADJECTIVES 87

CHAPTER 21: DEGREES OF ADJECTIVES 91

CHAPTER 22: ADVERBS 97

CHAPTER 23: PREPOSITION OR ADVERB? 101

CHAPTER 24: CONJUNCTIONS 103

CHAPTER 25: WHAT PART OF SPEECH IS THIS? 105

CHAPTER 26: SENTENCE 107

CHAPTER 27: SUBJECT AND PREDICATE 111

CHAPTER 28: COMPOUND SUBJECT AND COMPOUND PREDICATE 117

CHAPTER 29: SUBJECT-VERB AGREEMENT 119

CHAPTER 30: SPECIAL CASES – SUBJECT-VERB AGREEMENT 122

CHAPTER 31: SIMPLE, COMPOUND AND COMPLEX SENTENCES 125

CHAPTER 32: HOW TO USE COORDINATING CONJUNCTIONS 127

CHAPTER 33: COMPLEX SENTENCES 129

CHAPTER 34: SENTENCE ERRORS 131

CHAPTER 35: COMMA SPLICE 135

CHAPTER 36: SENTENCE FRAGMENT 137

CHAPTER 37: COMMON GRAMMATICAL ERRORS 141

CHAPTER 38: ERRORS WITH MODIFIERS 143

CHAPTER 39: CAPITALIZATION 147

CHAPTER 40: PUNCTUATION 151

CHAPTER 41: MORE ABOUT PUNCTUATION 155

CHAPTER 42: PARALLEL STRUCTURE 159

CHAPTER 43: WHO AND WHOM 161

CHAPTER 44: CONTRACTIONS 163

CHAPTER 45: SHORT REVIEW 167

CHAPTER 46: VOCABULARY BUILDING 169

CHAPTER 47: STRETCHING MY VOCABULARY 173

CHAPTER 48: SPELLING CHALLENGE 177

CHAPTER 49: SINGLE WORDS USED FOR PHRASES ... 181

CHAPTER 50: NEXT SECTION - BRINGING IT ALL TOGETHER.. 185

CHAPTER 51: INVENTION OF A POPULAR SPORT: BASKETBALL 187

CHAPTER 52: I DO AND I UNDERSTAND 199

MORE READING AVAILABLE 200

Chapter 1

PARTS OF SPEECH

In the past, you may have studied parts of speech in class and found it easy; or, maybe the concept sounded very confusing. The truth is, there is nothing mystifying about parts of speech. This is a friendly reminder that they are only the very foundation of the language that you use every day and that you take for granted.

Why is It Necessary to Learn Them?

Comprehension

Firstly, knowing your parts of speech will help in comprehension. Verbal or oral communication is enhanced through gestures. Written communication depends on correctly identifying the speaker and the person spoken to, and clarity of the message depends on the proper use of words. Parts of speech help us in making our message clear and to the point.

ABILITY TO DECIPHER

Secondly, in working with a difficult passage of prose, knowledge of parts of speech allows us to identify the different components of the writing, and can help us tease out the main points of the passage. For example, a passage may be so complex that we are unable after reading it to tell who the speaker is or what his or her message is. By being able to identify the subject and object of a sentence, we can identify what is being spoken about and what is being said about it. We can identify the action or 'being' words and tell what is happening in the passage.

BETTER WRITING

If we know the uses and functions of the various parts of speech, we can then communicate more effectively, and can even enhance our writing skills. We can then develop our own authentic voice through our writing, and will also be better equipped to self-correct when we write. We won't have to guess whether something that we wrote was grammatically correct or not.

WHAT ARE PARTS OF SPEECH?

Parts of speech are the basic classifications of the words that are used in language. In the English language, there are eight (8) parts of speech, namely, **nouns, verbs, pronouns, adjectives, adverbs, prepositions, conjunctions, and interjections.** This means that every word in the English language fits into one of these classifications. Think of parts of speech as neat categories for studying the language. When you write, you write in groups of words or sentences. By tackling the errors in your sentences according to the parts of speech involved, you will find that it is much easier to write correctly.

Parts of speech, errors in parts of speech, and sentences will be discussed below.

Chapter 2

WHAT IS A NOUN?

A noun is a word that is used to name a person, place, thing, idea, or action. It is the name given to anything. Examples are **book, table sun, John, Melissa, London, New York City, Toronto, university,** and **love**. There are different kinds of nouns. For example, there are **common nouns, proper nouns, concrete nouns, abstract nouns,** and **collective nouns.**

Kinds Of Nouns

Common Nouns

Common nouns are the names of common, everyday persons, places and things. Examples are **woman, roof, boy, store, building, shoe, athlete,** and **bag**.

Proper Nouns

Proper nouns are the names of particular persons, places, or things, and they are spelled with capital letters at the beginning of the words. Examples are **Silvia, Stephen,**

Montreal, the United States, Canada, Africa, California, Paris, Tobago, Istanbul, and **Asia.**

Concrete Nouns

Concrete nouns are names of things that can be seen and touched: Examples are **table, hat, juice, slippers, soda, hamburger, bus, building, automobile, station,** and **computer.**

Abstract Nouns

Abstract nouns are names of an idea, quality, or state of mind. Examples are **freedom, ignorance, happiness, integrity, love, education, democracy, terror,** and **honesty**.

Collective Nouns

Collective nouns are words that name a group of persons, places, or things. Examples are **team, choir, navy, army** and **population.**

WHAT IS A NOUN?

EXERCISE

In your notebook, make up your list of the different kinds of nouns shown below:

- **Common Nouns**
- **Proper Nouns**
- **Concrete Nouns**
- **Abstract Nouns**
- **Collective Nouns**

CHAPTER 3

NOUNS - SINGULAR AND PLURAL

Singular means one and plural means more than one. Singular and plural are used to identify the number of things.

To form the plural of most nouns, you would add 's' at the end of the singular form of the noun.

Examples of singular nouns are **girl, seminar, course, lecture, book,** and **plum.**

Examples of plural nouns where you **add 's' to the singular form** are **girls, seminars, courses, lectures, books,** and **plums.**

To form the plural of nouns ending with ch, s, sh, ss, x or z, you must add 'es' to the singular form of the nouns.

Examples of singular nouns ending with **ch, s, sh, ss, x,** and z are **church, bus, crash, glass, box, and buzz.**

NOUNS - SINGULAR AND PLURAL

Examples of plural nouns whose singular form has these endings are **churches, buses, crashes, glasses, boxes** and **buzzes.**

Reminder: Vowels are **a, e, i, o, u, and sometimes y.** Consonants are **all the other letters of the alphabet;** y sometimes functions **as a consonant.**

To form the plural of nouns ending with **'y' immediately preceded by a consonant**, you must **change the 'y' to an 'i' and add 'es'.**

Examples of singular nouns ending with **'y' immediately preceded by a consonant** are **baby, lily, candy,** and **lady.**

Examples of plural nouns whose singular form ends with **'y' immediately preceded by a consonant** are **babies, lilies, candies,** and **ladies.**

NOUNS - SINGULAR AND PLURAL

To form the plural of nouns ending with **'y' immediately preceded by a vowel**, you **would simply add 's' at the end of the singular form of the noun.**

Examples of singular nouns **ending with 'y' immediately preceded by a vowel** are **boy, toy,** and **play.**

Examples of plural nouns whose singular form **ends with 'y' immediately preceded by a vowel** are **boys, toys,** and **plays.**

To form the plural of nouns that end in **'o' preceded by a consonant**, you must add **'es.'**

Examples of singular nouns **ending in 'o' preceded by a consonant** are **potato, cargo, tomato, portico.**

Examples of plural nouns whose singular form **ends in 'o' preceded by a consonant** are **potatoes, cargoes, tomatoes,** and **porticoes.**

NOUNS - SINGULAR AND PLURAL

To form the plural of nouns ending in **o preceded by a vowel,** you would simply add **'s'**.

Examples of singular words ending in **o preceded by a vowel** are **video, cameo,** and **rodeo.**

Examples of plural words whose singular form ends in **o preceded by a vowel** are **videos, cameo,** and **rodeos.**

To form the plural of nouns **ending in 'f', change the 'f' to 'v', and add 'es'.** Examples of singular nouns **ending in 'f'** are **leaf, loaf, life, thief.**

Examples of plural nouns whose singular form **ends in 'f'** are **leaves, loaves, lives, thieves.**

It is important to note that while these are the basic rules, there are exceptions that you would encounter from time to time. For example, the plural of **chief** is **chiefs** and the plural of **brief** is **briefs.** In some of the other examples above, there are a few exceptions.

NOUNS - SINGULAR AND PLURAL

EXERCISE

Fill in the missing noun, either singular or plural. Write in your notebook.

Singular	Plural
Leaf	_____
Brief	_____
_____	Loaves
_____	Mangoes
Thief	_____
Video	_____
Player	_____
_____	Potatoes
Buzz	_____
_____	Candies
Church	_____
_____	Seminars

CHAPTER 4

UNUSUAL PLURALS

Some plurals do not follow the rules above in Chapter 3.

Some nouns remain the same in the singular and the plural.

Singular	**Plural**
One deer	Two deer
One sheep	Three sheep
One salmon	Many salmon
One spacecraft	Several spacecraft
One fish	Two fish
	(or fishes, when the word is used to mean two different kinds of fish)

For example:

Bass and perch are two different kinds of fish, or **Two fishes are bass and perch.**

UNUSUAL PLURALS

Some nouns change the word in the plural.

Singular	Plural
Child	Children
Foot	Feet
Goose	Geese
Man	Men
Woman	Women

Some nouns have two forms for the plural

Singular	Plural
Appendix	Appendixes, appendices (more commonly used)
Mosquito	Mosquitoes, mosquitos
Squash	Squash, squashes
Tornado	Tornadoes, tornados
Volcano	Volcanoes, volcanos

UNUSUAL PLURALS

Some nouns form the plural by changing the first part of the word.

Father-in-law   Fathers-in-law

Coat of arms   Coats of arms

Some nouns are only used in the plural form.

Examples of these nouns are **scissors, jeans, shorts, tights, and tongs.**

Some nouns are always used in the singular.

Examples of these nouns are **advice, information, furniture,** and **luggage.**

The men's **luggage is** in the bedroom.

Their **advice is** sound.

The **furniture is** beautiful.

UNUSUAL PLURALS

Some collective nouns, while they have a singular form, are considered plural.

Examples of these collective nouns are **people, cattle,** and **poultry.**

These people are my friends.

The cattle are in the truck.

Poultry are the farm's main product.

Some nouns have plurals, but retain the singular form when used collectively.

For example, you may say **one youth,** or **two youths,** when referring to **individuals.** When referring to a **group,** you may say **youth.**

One youth is coming to Canada.

Three youths are going on the trip to Africa.

Youth are expected to stay behind and help.

UNUSUAL PLURALS

Some nouns that end in 's' are really singular.

Examples of these nouns are **electronics, news, mathematics** and **physics.**

The news is usually at 6 p.m.

Mathematics is not a difficult subject.

Physics is the subject after biology.

UNUSUAL PLURALS

EXERCISE

Complete the exercise below. (Write in your notebook). Where the singular is given, put in the plural. Where the plural is given, fill in the singular

Singular	Plural
Coat of arms	___
Goose	___
Appendix	___
Salmon	
Woman	Women
Deer	
Sheep	___
Child	___
___	Feet
Squash	___
Sister-in-law	___
One youth	Three ___
___	Trout

Complete your own singular and plural nouns below in your notebook.

Chapter 5

NOUNS SHOWING POSSESSION

(Possessive Case)

In order to show possession, nouns are used in the possessive case.

Possession, meaning 'belonging to', is shown by using the noun followed by apostrophe 's'.

For example, **'this book belongs to John'** or **'This is John's book'**. **John's** is in the possessive case.

The bat belonging to Carl	Carl's bat
The bowl belonging to the dog	the dog's bowl
The house belonging to the girls	the girls' house
The ball belonging to Charlene	Charlene's ball
The plan belonging to the team	the team's plan
This menu belongs to café	the café's menu
This copy belongs to the teacher	the teacher's copy
The robes belong to the choir	the choir's robes

EXERCISE

Correct the following: Write in your notebook.

1. The children are going to Marthas house.

2. Martha is going to the childrens home.

CHAPTER 6

DO NOT FORM PLURALS USING THE APOSTROPHE

DO NOT SAY: "There were two boy's in the room."

This is wrong. You should write: "There were two boys in the room."

Explanation:

"boys" refer to more than one boy

"boy's" means "belonging to the boy".

There are only two cases when you can use apostrophes:

1. Use apostrophe to show possession, when something belongs to someone. For example, you would say "This is John's hat", meaning that the hat belongs to John.
2. Use when something is omitted, for example, "She didn't see the movie." In this last sentence, you could have said, "She did not see the movie," but you can omit the 'o' from 'did not' and write 'didn't'.

DO NOT FORM PLURALS USING THE APOSTROPHE

EXERCISE

1. Make up your own sentences using apostrophes to show possession or where something is omitted or left out. Write in your notebook.

2. Overcoming major error with the use of apostrophe. Indicate whether True (T) or False (F). Write in your notebook.

   ____ The boy's bicycle is in the garage.

   ____ The boy's are coming home tonight.

   ____ They weren't going to school today.

   ____ The doctor's were at the conference for the day.

   ____ Jen and Kelly didnot go to the seminar.

CHAPTER 7

VERBS

VERBS are words that denote a state of being or an action. In other words, verbs tell the state that something is in or describes an action that takes place.

For Example:

He is an athlete. (state of being)

They are sisters. (state of being)

We are happy. (state of being)

The professor gave a surprise quiz. (action)

The children ate the pizza. (action)

The kitten played with the ball of thread. (action)

Examples of state of being verbs are: is, are, become, feel.

Examples of action words: run, buy, contact, evaporate.

TYPES OF VERBS

There are three main types of verbs: Transitive verbs, Intransitive verbs, and Linking verbs.

(1) Transitive verbs

Transitive verbs are action words that transfer the action from the subject to the object. Transitive verbs take an object. (Clue: to find out if a verb has an object, ask the question 'what?')

For example:

The boy **ate** the apple. (The action passes from the subject, 'the boy', to the object, 'the apple'.)

(Clue: Ask to yourself, "The boy ate "what"? The answer is 'apple', so 'apple' is the object.) The action passed from the boy to the apple. 'Ate' in this sentence is a transitive verb.

VERBS

The children <u>brought</u> their books.

The verb 'brought' takes 'books' as object. The action passed from the children to books.

'Brought' is a transitive verb.

CHAPTER 8

TYPES OF VERBS (Continued)

(2) Intransitive verbs

Intransitive verbs are action words that do not transfer action to an object. Intransitive verbs do not have objects.

For example:

The children <u>laughed</u>. (The action, 'laughed', stays with 'The children'.)

(Clue: Ask yourself: "The children laughed what?". You get no answer, and you know there is no object.)

"Laughed" is an intransitive verb.

TYPES OF VERBS (Continued)

The president <u>departed.</u> (The action, 'departed', stays with 'The president'.)

(Clue: Ask yourself: "The president departed 'what'? You get no answer.)

The verb 'departed' has no object.

'Departed' is an intransitive verb.

Note: Some verbs can be used as transitive verbs and as intransitive verbs.

An example is the verb 'sing'.

The boy can **sing** the song. ('sing' is transitive because it carries the action forward from the '**boy**' to '**song**'.

The boy can **sing**. ('sing' is intransitive because it does not have an object).

Write some sentences with intransitive verbs in your notebook.

CHAPTER 9

TYPES OF VERBS (Continued)

(3) Linking verbs

Linking verbs are verbs that do not show action, but represent a state of being.

For Example:

She is a dentist.

The head is part of the body.

Teaching is a profession.

The verb 'is' is a linking verb.

Other Linking Verbs

Several other linking verbs that are commonly used are appear, be, grow, look, remain, seem, smell, stay and taste. All of these linking verbs serve to join the subject with a word that describes the subject.

Jonathan **appears** sad today.

The flowers **smell** sweet.

The meal **tastes** delicious.

TYPES OF VERBS (Continued)

EXERCISE

Write in your notebook.

1. Review the different types of verbs.

2. Make up 10 sentences that include transitive verbs.

3. Make up 10 sentences that include intransitive verbs.

4. Make up 10 sentences that include linking verbs.

CHAPTER 10

TENSES AND VERB FORMS

Verbs have four main forms: the present, the present participle, the past, and the past participle. These forms are used to create different verb tenses.

Verbs are also regular and irregular. Regular verbs are conjugated or are changed into the four verb forms using a consistent pattern. For example, the verb "play" is a regular verb because it follows a consistent pattern in its four verb forms. The present tense form is "dance"; the present participle form is "dancing"; the past form is "danced"; and the past participle form is "danced".

Irregular verbs are conjugated or are changed into the four verb forms in an inconsistent pattern. For example, the verb "run" is an irregular verb because it follows an inconsistent pattern in its four verb forms. The present tense form is "run"; the present participle form is "running"; the past form is "ran"; and the past participle form is "run".

REGULAR VERBS

These verbs have a basic structure. These verbs make up the majority of verbs and follow a simple pattern for these four forms of the verb.

Here are some examples below.

Present Form	Present Participle	Past Form	Past Participle
Offer	Offering	offered	offered
Play	Playing	Played	Played

EXAMPLES OF USE

We **offer** our gifts to the children. **(Present form)**

We are **offering** our gifts to the children. **(Present Participle)**

We **offered** our gifts to the children. **(Past form)**

We have **offered** our gifts to the children. **(Past participle)**

The children **play** in the park. **(Present form)**

The children are **playing** in the park. **(Present Participle)**

The children **played** in the park. **(Past form)**

The children have **played** in the park. **(Past participle)**

IRREGULAR VERBS - SOME IRREGULAR VERB FORMS

Present Form	Present Participle	Past Form	Past Participle
Break	Breaking	Broke	Broken
Bring	Bringing	Brought	Brought
Buy	Buying	Bought	Bought
Choose	Choosing	Chose	Chosen
Do	Doing	Did	Done
Drink	Drinking	Drank	Drunk
Eat	Eating	Ate	Eaten
Fly	Flying	Flew	Flown
Freeze	Freezing	Froze	Frozen
Know	Knowing	Knew	Known
Ride	Riding	Rode	Ridden
Run	Running	Ran	Run
Throw	Throwing	Threw	Thrown

However, there are other tenses between the past and present. These verb forms were shown to form the present and the past above. In the next chapter, we will explore the use of these four verb forms to form different tenses, or to indicate when the action takes place.

CHAPTER 11

FORMING TENSES

Note: Forms of the word 'be' and 'have' are used as 'helping verbs' in forming tenses.

VERB TENSES

There are several verb tenses that will be discussed and illustrated below. These are the Present Tense, Past Tense, Future Tense, Present Progressive Tense, Present Perfect Tense, Past Perfect tense, and Future Perfect Tense.

Present Tense

Present action or state of being - I **play** the piano.

Past Tense

Past action that is completed – I **played** the piano yesterday.

Future Tense

Action that will take place in the future – I **will play** the piano tomorrow.

Present Progressive Tense

Action that is still taking place in the present – I **am playing** the piano right now.

Present Perfect Tense

Action that started in the past and still continues to take place – I **have played** the piano every day this month.

Past Perfect Tense

Action that took place in the past and that was completed before a particular time in the past – I **had played** the piano before it was destroyed.

Future Perfect Tense

Action that will be completed by a particular time in the future – I will have played the piano for two hours by the time the concert begins.

EXERCISE

Try making sentences using the various tenses discussed above. Write in your notebook.

CHAPTER 12

SOME PROBLEM VERBS

LAY AND **LIE** are verbs that are often confused.

The Verb "LAY"

Verb	Past	Participle
Lay	laid	laid

'Lay' is a transitive verb and so takes an object.

He laid the book on the desk.

The verb 'laid' takes 'book' as object. (laid is past tense of 'lay)

The girl lays her bag on the seat.

The verb 'lays' takes 'bag' as object. (lays is the present tense of lay)

The Verb "LIE"

Verb	Past	Participle
Lie	lay	lain

SOME PROBLEM VERBS

'Lie' is an intransitive verb and so does not take an object.

The child <u>lies</u> on his bed all day. **(Clue: 'lies' what – there is no answer)**

The verb 'lies' has no object.

The cat <u>lay</u> in the corner.

This verb 'lay' is the past tense of lie.

'Lay' in this sentence is intransitive and does not take an object.

Note: Do not confuse the verb 'lay' (present tense of the transitive verb 'lay') with 'lay' (past tense of the intransitive verb 'lie').

CHAPTER 13

MORE PROBLEM VERBS

RAISE AND **RISE** are verbs that are often confused.

The Verb "RAISE"

Verb	Past	Participle
Raise	raised	raised

'Raise' is always a transitive verb and so takes an object.

He <u>raised</u> the curtains and looked outside.

The verb 'raised' takes 'curtains' as object.

They <u>raised</u> their voices in song.

The verb 'raised' takes 'voices' as object.

MORE PROBLEM VERBS

The Verb "RISE"

Verb	Past	Participle
Rise	rose	risen

'Rise' is always an intransitive verb and so does not take an object.

The sun <u>rises</u>.

The verb 'rise' has no object.

When the anthem played, the children <u>rose.</u>

The verb 'rose' has no object. (**'rose'** is past tense of **'rise'**)

EXERCISE

Make sentences in your notebook, **using 'lay' and 'lie' and 'raise' and 'rise'.**

CHAPTER 14

MORE PROBLEM VERBS

SET AND SIT

These are also words that are often misused and confused.

THE VERB "SET"

Verb	Past	Participle
Set	set	set

'Set' is a transitive verb and so takes an object.

The teacher <u>set</u> the atlas on her desk.

The verb 'set' takes 'atlas' as object.

Note: 'Set' could also be an intransitive verb in the following example:

The sun <u>sets.</u>

THE VERB "SIT"

Verb	Past	Participle
Sit	sat	sat

'Sit' is an intransitive verb and so does not take an object. (Clue: 'sit' what – there is no answer)

I often sit in the library and read.

The man sat on the couch.

CHAPTER 15

MORE PROBLEM VERBS

BORROW AND LEND

These two verbs are sometimes confused and used incorrectly.

'Borrow' refers to act of receiving something.

'Lend' refers to the act of giving something.

They are both transitive verbs, but the difference between the verbs are in their meanings.

For example:

My friend **borrows** money **from** the bank. (Clue: **borrow from)**

The bank **lends** money **to** my friend. (Clue: **lend to**)

LEARN AND TEACH

'Learn' refers to the act of receiving something.

'Teach' refers to the act of giving something.

For Example:

I **learned** my lessons. (Clue: **meaning of acquiring knowledge**)

My mother **teaches** music. (Clue: **meaning of educating or giving knowledge**)

The expression, "That will learn you" is grammatically incorrect and sometimes said in jest, but is never considered acceptable.

EXERCISE

Write in your notebook. Make 10 sentences using the words 'sit' and 'set', 10 using 'borrow' and 'lend', and 10 using 'learn' and 'teach'.

Chapter 16

OTHER FORMS OF VERBS – VERBALS

Verbals are words that are derived from verbs and that are used as nouns and adjectives. Three types of verbals are the infinitive, gerund, and participle or verbal adjective.

Infinitive

One type of verbal is the infinitive or the 'to be' part of the verb.

Examples of infinitives are: **to make, to do, to be, to run, to read.**

Gerund

Another type of verbal is the gerund or verbal noun. This verbal noun ends in 'ing'. Examples of gerunds are: **running, standing, reading.**

OTHER FORMS OF VERBS – VERBALS

PARTICIPLE OR VERBAL ADJECTIVE

Another type of verbal is the participle or verbal adjective. This verbal adjective usually ends in - ed. Examples of participles or verbal adjectives are: **returned, arrived, ruled, believed.**

Use of Verbals as Nouns and Adjective

Verbals are verb forms that can be used as nouns or can be used as adjectives.

The infinitive and gerund, two of the verbal forms, are generally used as nouns.

The participle, the third verbal form, is used as an adjective. See the examples below.

Infinitive as Verbal Noun

<u>To study</u> hard is rewarding.

('To study' is the infinitive, and here it is used as a noun).

OTHER FORMS OF VERBS – VERBALS

Gerund as Verbal Noun

Running can be fun.

Participle as Verbal Adjective

Exhausted, the athlete collapsed.

Verbals as Introductory Modifiers

These verbal nouns and adjectives are also known as verbal modifiers.

Introductory Verbal Modifier

An Introductory verbal modifier should immediately come before the noun that it modifies. See examples of how this is used.

Returning from a trip, **Ronald** met his long-time friend. The introductory verbal modifier, "returning", modifies the noun 'Ronald' and so comes immediately before 'Ronald'.

Coming back from the movies, the **guests** were standing in the lobby.

The introductory verbal modifier, 'coming back', modifies the noun 'guests'.

CAUTION – MAJOR ERRORS – VERY COMMON

If this sentence were written in the following way, it would be **incorrect:**

Coming back from the movies, there were guests standing in the lobby. (incorrect)

This sentence is wrong because the introductory verbal modifier, 'coming back', does not come immediately before 'guests'.

CHAPTER 17

INFINITIVE OF PURPOSE

An Infinitive of Purpose may be used as an introductory modifier.

Make sure a verb follows the infinitive of purpose.

For example:

<u>**To give a good impression**</u>, **speak** clearly.

The verb 'speak' follows the infinitive of purpose, 'to give a good impression'.

<u>**To play well**</u>, **use** the appropriate equipment.

The verb 'use' follows the infinitive of purpose, 'to play well'.

(The infinitive of purpose is separated from the rest of the sentence by a comma.)

EXERCISE

Make 10 sentences using the infinitive of purpose. **Write in your notebook.**

CHAPTER 18

PRONOUNS

A pronoun is a word that stands in place of a noun or replaces a noun.

The noun that it replaces is called the antecedent.

Examples of pronouns are **she, he, him, they, you, us, and we.**

The **children** went to the movies – **They** went to the movies.

'Children" is the antecedent or the noun that is being replaced by the pronoun "they".

DIFFERENT TYPES OF PRONOUNS

Personal pronouns - she, he, they, you.

Possessive pronouns - his, her, hers, mine, my, our, theirs, its.

Interrogative pronouns - who, whom, what, which.

Reflexive pronouns - myself, yourself, himself.

Relative pronouns - who, whose, which, that.

Indefinite Pronouns

Indefinite pronouns are pronouns that refer to an unnamed person and could be either singular or plural. Singular indefinite pronouns are each, one, everyone, everybody, no one, nobody, anybody, anyone, somebody, and someone. Plural indefinite pronouns are both, many, several and few.

Demonstrative pronouns – that, this, those, these

Demonstrative pronouns point out specific people or things.

'This' and 'these' refer to things close by. 'That' and 'those' refer to specific people or persons that are distant.

Pronouns used only as Subjective Case and as Objective Case

PRONOUNS

Some pronouns are only used as the subject.

Examples of pronouns as subjects are: I, we, they, he, she, who.

Use in sentence: We went to the movies. **'We'** is the subject of the sentence.

They had several lessons this week. **'They'** is the subject of the sentence.

Some pronouns are only used as the object.

Examples of pronouns as objects are: me, us, them, him, her, whom.

Use in sentence.

John took **them** home. **'Them'** is the object, or what John took home.

TO CLARIFY

You will never say: **'Us'** went to the movies, because **'us'** is a pronoun that is only used as the **object**. You would say, **'We'** went to the movies, because **'we'** is a pronoun that is always used as the **subject**.

EXERCISE

Write 5 each of the different types of pronouns in your notebook. **Make sentences including them.**

Chapter 19

PRONOUN-ANTECEDENT AGREEMENT

The antecedent and the pronoun that replaces it must agree in number and person. If the antecedent is singular, then the pronoun that replaces it must be singular. If the antecedent is plural, then the pronoun that replaces it must also be plural.

All this means is that if you use a noun in one sentence and then use a pronoun in a following sentence to stand for the noun in the first sentence, both the noun and the pronoun in the first and second sentences must agree.

PRONOUN-ANTECEDENT AGREEMENT

For example:

Harry bought the book. It was very interesting.

'Book' in the first sentence is the antecedent of 'it' in the second sentence. If the pronoun 'it' was not used, the sentences would have read: Harry bought the book. The book was very interesting. This is why 'book' and 'it' have to agree in number and person.

To show that the antecedent and the pronoun must agree, let us look at the sentences again.

Harry bought the book. They were very interesting.

This is wrong because 'book' is singular or just one thing, while the pronoun 'they' refers to many things.

PRONOUN-ANTECEDENT AGREEMENT

Let us look at the sentences again. This time they are changed a little.

Harry bought the books. They were very interesting.

This is right, because the noun 'books' in the first sentence agrees with 'they' in the second sentence as both are plural.

Here's another example of pronoun-antecedent agreement.

The student made two documentaries last month. They won the award.

'Documentaries' is the antecedent of 'They', because it was the documentaries that won the award.

The student made two documentaries last month. It won the award.

This would be wrong, because 'documentaries' is plural, and 'it', which is intended to refer to 'documentaries', is singular.

Therefore, the pronoun and its antecedent must agree in number.

CAUTION: It is important in avoiding confusion as to which word is the antecedent and this can be dealt with by repeating the noun.

For example, look at the sentence below. It is a variant of one of the sentences above.

The student made **two documentaries** last month. **It** won the award.

This sentence is wrong, because there is no agreement between the pronoun and its antecedent: "it" and "documentaries" - "documentaries" is plural and "it" is singular.

PRONOUN-ANTECEDENT AGREEMENT

Look at this sentence:

The students made two documentaries last month. They won the award.

"Documentaries" is plural and "they" is plural. But the meaning of this sentence may not clear, because "they" could refer to the "students" as well as to "documentaries".

In this case, in order to be clear about the meaning, write:

"The students made two documentaries last month and the documentaries won the award" (if it were the documentaries that won the award).

However, if it is the students who won the award, the sentence would be different.

"The students made two documentaries last month, and the students won the award."

Pronoun-Antecedent Agreement with Collective Nouns

Collective nouns (such as army, team) take the singular pronoun 'it'.

It is important to take note that collective nouns are treated as singular. When we speak of a 'team', although a team consists of many people, it is still just one 'team'. The 'team' has to be treated as singular.

The **team** paid for the renovations to the locker room. **They** were required to do so. **(Error in agreement)**

The correct form of the sentence should be as follows:

The **team** paid for the renovations to the locker room. **It** was required to do so. **(Correct)**

Team is a collective noun and so is treated as a singular noun. 'It' is also singular.

Another common error that involves the antecedent and the pronoun is that they must agree in person. The antecedent and the pronoun that replaces it must agree in person.

PRONOUN-ANTECEDENT AGREEMENT

The antecedent and the pronoun that replaces it are in agreement, when they are **both in the first person, that is, referring to the speaker; in the second person, that is, referring to the person spoken to;** or **in the third person, that is, referring to the person spoken about.**

For Example:

James went to university in September. **He** was pleased to be accepted.

'James' is the antecedent of 'He'.

The **children** went to the circus. **They** were very happy.

'Children' is the antecedent of **'they'**.

Errors in Antecedent-Pronoun Agreement (Person)
If <u>one</u> studies hard, <u>you</u> could expect to succeed. (Error in Agreement)

If <u>you</u> study hard, <u>you</u> could expect to succeed. (Correct)

If <u>one</u> studies hard, <u>one</u> could expect to succeed. (Correct)

PRONOUN-ANTECEDENT AGREEMENT

If <u>one</u> studies hard, <u>he or she</u> could expect to succeed. (Correct)

These are three different ways to correct this same sentence.

The important point to bear in mind is that the antecedent and its corresponding pronoun must always agree in person and number.

EXERCISE: Take notes in your notebook.

For Clarity

When a pronoun is used, there must be no doubt about the antecedent.

The man came with his son. He was very happy to be at the meeting. (Unclear)

One is not clear whether the pronoun 'He" refers to the 'man' or his 'son'.

Therefore, the noun must be repeated for clarity.

The sentence should be corrected so that it is clear who is 'happy'.

The man came with his son. His son was very happy to be at the meeting.

The sentence can also be corrected with a change in construction.

The man came with his son, who was very happy to be at the meeting.

If it was the man that was happy, then the sentences should read:

The man came with his son. The man was very happy to be at the meeting.

CHAPTER 20

ADJECTIVES

ADJECTIVES

An adjective is a descriptive word, used with a noun or pronoun.

Examples of adjectives are **black, sweet, happy, big, heavy.**

Usually, adjectives come before nouns, as in <u>black</u> cherry, <u>sweet</u> flavour, <u>happy</u> person, <u>big</u> bundle, <u>heavy</u> bag.

There are different types of adjectives:
There are predicate adjectives, demonstrative adjectives and possessive adjectives.

PREDICATE ADJECTIVES

There are times when an adjective comes after the noun or pronoun that it describes. An adjective might appear in the predicate.

For example:

She is <u>strong</u>. Harry is <u>happy</u>.

"Strong" and "happy" are predicate adjectives, as they are part of the predicate or the verb part of the sentence.

DEMONSTRATIVE ADJECTIVES

Two demonstrative adjectives are 'this' (for singular) and 'these' (for plural), and they refer to things that are close.

For example:

He bought <u>this</u> bat and <u>these</u> balls. (close by)

The other two demonstrative adjectives are 'that' (for singular) and 'those' (for plural), and they refer to things that are distant.

For example:

She brought <u>that</u> book and <u>those</u> pencils. (at a distance)

POSSESSIVE ADJECTIVES:

These are adjectives that indicate ownership or show possession. Some possessive adjectives are **your, my, their, his, her, our, its.**

For example:

<u>My</u> friend is coming home.

<u>Your</u> hat is on the ground.

<u>Their</u> house is just around the corner.

OTHER ERRORS IN ANTECEDENT-POSSESSIVE ADJECTIVE AGREEMENT (NUMBER)

Another common error that involves antecedent and possessive adjective agreement is seen in the examples below. Since the possessive adjective is also a form of the pronoun, this kind of error is sometimes also referred to as **an antecedent-pronoun agreement error.**

For example:

Any **student** can bring **their** laptop to school. **(Error in agreement)**

The noun **'student'** is singular but the possessive pronoun **'their'** is plural. Therefore, this is a common error that must be corrected.

Any **student** can bring **his or her** laptop to school. **(Correct)**

CHAPTER 21

DEGREES OF ADJECTIVES

Adjectives can be used to compare things. **Adjectives are therefore said to differ in degree.**

A bag can be described as being **heavy,** but another bag can be described as **heavier**, and a third bag can be described as **the heaviest**. These differ in degree. Therefore, **adjectives can be either positive,** when one speaks of one thing only; **comparative,** when two things are compared; **or superlative,** when three or more things are compared.

Positive	**Comparative**	**Superlative**
Big	Bigger	Biggest
Red	Redder	Reddest
Late	Later	Latest

DEGREES OF ADJECTIVES

For example:

John is big. ('Big' is in the positive degree.)

John is bigger than his brother.

('Bigger' is in the comparative degree.)

John is the biggest in the class.

('Biggest' is in the superlative degree.)

Other examples are as follows:

One building is high.

This building is higher than the other.

The third building is the highest.

Paul is tall.

Tamara is taller than Paul.

Ray is the tallest of the three children.

The rule is that when one thing is described, and no comparison is made, the positive degree is used. **Examples of adjectives in the positive degree are big, high, tall.**

DEGREES OF ADJECTIVES

When two things are described and compared, the comparative degree is used. This is usually done by adding '-er' to the word. **Examples are bigger, higher, taller.**

When three or more things are described and compared, the superlative degree is used. This is usually done by adding '-est' to the word. **Examples are biggest, highest, tallest. The Use of 'more' and 'most' in describing and comparing things.**

In some cases, one cannot change the positive to the comparative and the superlative degrees by adding **'er' or 'est'**. In these circumstances, one must add **'more' and most**.

For example:

The word 'beautiful' cannot be changed by adding 'er' or 'est'.

It can be changed as follows:

Positive	**Comparative**	**Superlative**
Beautiful	More beautiful	Most beautiful

DEGREES OF ADJECTIVES

Examples in using 'more' and 'most' in comparisons are as follows.

The forest was a beautiful scene.

The city was a more beautiful scene.

The sunset was the most beautiful scene.

Use of Different Words for the comparative and superlative forms

There are times when making comparisons involves using different words for the positive, comparative, and superlative degrees.

In some cases, the comparative and superlative forms of the adjective change altogether. This is the case with the words 'good' and 'bad'.

DEGREES OF ADJECTIVES

Positive	Comparative	Superlative
Good	better	best
Bad	worse	worst

For example:

Ronald is a good runner.

Steve is a better runner than Ronald.

Dave is the best runner on the team.

The movie was bad.

That movie was worse.

This was the worst movie.

CAUTION: Never say "more better" or "more bad". These are definitely wrong, although commonly used.

Chapter 22

ADVERBS

ADVERBS are words that modify verbs, adjectives or other adverbs. They usually describe when, where, why, to what extent and how. Some adverbs are: happily, carefully, smoothly, today, outside.

For example:
The children played <u>happily</u>.
The divers worked <u>carefully.</u>
We went to the museum <u>early</u>.

While most adverbs end in 'ly', adverbs are words that also answer questions such as 'how', 'when', 'where', and 'to what degree'.

Degrees of Adverbs

Like adjectives, adverbs could have degrees. They are usually represented by the use of 'more' and 'most'.

Positive	Comparative	Superlative
Slowly	more slowly	most slowly
Carefully	more carefully	most carefully.

Adverbs and Prepositions are often confused, so there would be more details about adverbs when explaining about prepositions below.

PREPOSITIONS

A preposition is a word that shows the relation of its object to some other word, usually a verb, in the sentence.

For example:

The boy ran **across** the field.

(In this sentence, 'across' is the preposition, 'field' is the object of the preposition, and 'across' shows the relation of 'field' to 'ran').

The car travelled under the bridge.

(In this sentence, 'under' is the preposition, 'bridge' is the object of the preposition, and 'under' shows the relation of 'bridge' to 'travelled'.)

Here are some other examples:

The plane flew over the parade.

The children stayed outside of the house.

Note: Prepositions always occur in a prepositional phrase. In the examples above, under the bridge, over the parade, and outside of the house are all prepositional phrases, introduced by the prepositions under, over and outside, respectively.

CHAPTER 23

PREPOSITION OR ADVERB?

Prepositions and adverbs are often confused. one word can be a preposition or an adverb, depending on how that word appears in the sentence.

'OUTSIDE' AS PREPOSITION

The children stayed <u>outside</u> of the house. **(Preposition)**

In this sentence, the word **'outside'** has an object, **'house'**, and so in this context, **<u>outside</u> is a <u>preposition</u>**.

(A preposition can be said to introduce an adverb prepositional phrase, and it answers the question 'where'. The answer is the whole phrase, "outside of the house".

Where did the children stay? The answer is, "outside of the house". 'Outside" has the object, 'house', in this case.

'OUTSIDE' AS ADVERB

The children stayed <u>outside</u>. (adverb)

In this sentence, **<u>'outside'</u> does not have an object, and so is an <u>adverb</u>.**

It answers the question 'where?' with only one word, 'outside'. Where did the children stay? The answer is 'outside'.

CHAPTER 24

CONJUNCTIONS

A conjunction is a word that joins words, phrases, or clauses.

For example:

The children <u>and</u> their friends were tired.

The work in the lab <u>and</u> in the office must be done.

The boy went home, <u>but</u> the girl went to school.

INTERJECTIONS

An interjection is a word that expresses strong feeling or emotion.

For example:

<u>Great</u>! I made it!

<u>Wow</u>! What a show!

CHAPTER 25

WHAT PART OF SPEECH IS THIS?

Some words can be used as different parts of speech. Let us look at the word **'home'**. It can be different parts of speech, depending on how it is used.

I bought a <u>home</u>. (noun)

When the question is asked 'bought what', the answer is 'home'.

I went <u>home</u>. (adverb)

When the question is asked 'went where', the answer is 'home'. Therefore, 'home' in this context is an adverb.

The guided missiles <u>home in</u> on their targets. (verb)

When the question is asked about the action of the 'guided missiles', the answer is that they 'home in' or carried out this action.

WHAT PART OF SPEECH IS THIS?

The students ate <u>home</u> fries and hotdogs for lunch. (adjective)

In this sentence, 'home' is an adjective, because it describes the kinds of 'fries' that the 'students ate'.

Run

She can <u>run</u> very fast. (verb)

She made a home <u>run.</u> (noun)

Fast

They are <u>fast</u> runners. (adjective)

They can run <u>fast</u>. (adverb)

EXERCISE

Write in your notebook any words you can think of that can be used as different parts of speech.

CHAPTER 26

SENTENCE

Sentence: A sentence is a group of words that express a complete thought. **There are four kinds of sentences, namely, declaratory, interrogative, imperative and exclamatory. All sentences end with a punctuation mark, indicating that it is a complete thought.**

KINDS OF SENTENCES

A Declaratory sentence is a sentence that makes a statement.

   Today is Monday.

   John brought his friend.

This kind of sentence ends with a full stop or a period.

An Interrogative sentence is a sentence that asks a question.

    Where are you going?

    Why did you come?

An interrogatory question ends with a question mark.

An Imperative sentence gives a command or makes a request.

    Please hand me my books.

    Get out of here!

This kind of sentence ends with a period or an exclamation mark.

The fourth kind of sentence is an exclamatory sentence.

An Exclamatory sentence is one that makes a request or gives a command with strong feeling.

    What a pleasant day we had!

    It's a winner!

Exclamatory sentences end with an exclamation mark, and expresses strong feeling.

In the case of the imperative sentence, a period is used if a request is made. However, if the imperative sentence involves giving a command, then an exclamation mark must be used to express strong feeling.

EXERCISE

In your notebook, write 10 declaratory, 10 interrogatory, 10 imperative, and 10 exclamatory sentences.

Chapter 27

SUBJECT AND PREDICATE

Each sentence is made up of a subject and a predicate.

John	completed his work quickly.
Subject	**Predicate**

Basically, the subject can be a noun or a noun clause (group of words with a noun in it) which refers to the person or the thing which does the action.

In the sentence above, the noun is 'John' and the action that John did was that he "completed his work quickly".

Therefore, **'John' is the subject** and **'completed his work quickly'** is the predicate.

But there are times when we may be asked to identify the bare subject and the bare predicate.

In the sentence above, John completed his work quickly, 'John' is the bare subject and 'completed' is the bare predicate.

If we were asked to identify the subject and the predicate or the full subject and the full predicate, then we would identify 'John' as the full subject and 'completed his work quickly' as the full predicate.

Note: If we were asked to identify the subject and the predicate, we would identify the full subject and the full predicate.

Let's take another sentence:

The hungry children ate their pizza quickly.

Simple Subject or Bare Subject

A simple subject is the person or thing that the sentence is about.

The hungry **children** ate their pizza quickly.

SIMPLE SUBJECT

In the sentence above, the bare subject is the noun that refers to the person or persons taking the action.

The bare subject or the simple subject is 'children'.

SIMPLE PREDICATE OR BARE PREDICATE

A simple predicate tells the bare minimum that pertains to the subject.

The hungry children **ate** their pizza quickly.

SUBJECT AND PREDICATE

SIMPLE PREDICATE

If we were asked to identify the bare predicate or the simple predicate in the sentence above, we would say **'ate'**.

Therefore, in the sentence: The hungry children ate their pizza quickly, **the bare subject or simple subject is 'children' and the bare predicate or simple predicate is 'ate'.**

In other words, the bare subject and bare predicate would read:

                Children   ate.
        (Simple Subject) (Simple Predicate)

If we were asked to identify the subject and predicate or the complete subject and complete predicate, we would indicate, **'The hungry children". A complete subject tells everything that describes the subject.** The sentence points out that the children were hungry.

SUBJECT AND PREDICATE

A complete predicate tells everything that pertains to the subject. In this sentence, the complete predicate is 'ate their pizza quickly'.

<u>**The hungry children**</u>　　<u>**ate their pizza quickly**</u>.
　Complete subject　　　　　　Complete Predicate

EXERCISE

In your notebook, underline the bare subject and circle the bare predicate in the sentences below.

1. Several visitors went to the museum.
2. University students prepare for their exams.
3. The musical director chose the songs for the concert.
4. The strict principal reprimanded the students for being late.

CHAPTER 28

COMPOUND SUBJECT AND COMPOUND PREDICATE

COMPOUND SUBJECT

A compound subject has two or more subjects. For example, in the sentence below, it is not only 'the hungry children' but also 'their parents' that are the subject of the sentence.

<u>The hungry children and their parents</u> ate the pizza quickly.

The compound subject in this sentence is "The hungry children and their parents".

COMPOUND PREDICATE

A compound predicate has two or more predicates.

The predicate is not only 'ate their pizza quickly' but they also 'left right away'.

The hungry children and their parents <u>**ate their pizza quickly and left right away**</u>.

COMPOUND SUBJECT AND COMPOUND PREDICATE

Therefore, this sentence has a compound subject and a compound predicate.

'The hungry children and their parents' – (Compound Subject.)

'ate their pizza quickly and left right away'- (Compound predicate)

Chapter 29

SUBJECT-VERB AGREEMENT

The subject and verb must agree in number. If the subject is singular, then the verb must agree with the singular noun. If the subject is plural, the verb must also agree with the plural noun.

(This is an area that is always tested. It is very easy to make a mistake here).

It is important to understand the importance of the 'bare subject' and be able to identify it.

For example:

One of the children <u>play</u> the piano. (Incorrect)

This is incorrect because the subject is singular and so must have a verb that agrees with a singular subject.

In this sentence, the subject is 'one'.

'One' is singular and so must take the form of the verb that agrees with a singular noun.

SUBJECT-VERB AGREEMENT

But in the sentence above, 'play' is the form of the verb that agrees with a plural noun. Therefore, 'play' is incorrect in the sentence above.

The verb must agree with the singular noun and so must be '<u>plays</u>'.

One of the children <u>plays</u> the piano. (Correct)

Note: The subject of a sentence is never in a prepositional phrase, and so 'children' could not be the subject.

Also, remember how to conjugate the verb 'play':

I <u>play</u>

You <u>play</u>

He, she or it <u>plays</u>

We <u>play</u>

You <u>play</u>

They <u>play</u>

SUBJECT-VERB AGREEMENT

You add 's' to make a noun plural; but you take away an 's' when you form a verb that agrees with a plural noun.

The boys play.

The boy plays.

EXERCISE

In your notebook, correct the following sentences and explain why they need correction.

1. The girls runs in the marathon races.

2. Jonathan make a delicious meal for his parents.

Chapter 30

SPECIAL CASES – SUBJECT-VERB AGREEMENT

CAUTION – Major errors are made here.

When the words ending in 'one', 'thing', or ' body', and the word 'each', are used as subjects, they are treated as singular, and so take the verb forms that agree with the singular pronouns.

For example:

Each one of the monkeys **eats** its banana.

Everyone has a hat.

Anyone uses the keys.

When the words 'few', 'both', 'several' and 'many' are used as pronouns, they are considered plural.

SPECIAL CASES – SUBJECT-VERB AGREEMENT

Plural verb forms must agree with pronouns that are in the plural.

Few of them **have** cell phones.

Both of the children **have** books.

Several of them **are** in the library.

Many of the animals **were** released.

CHAPTER 31

SIMPLE, COMPOUND AND COMPLEX SENTENCES

Sentences could also be **simple, compound or complex**.

SIMPLE SENTENCES

A simple sentence has one independent clause.

For example:

> **Sue bought a pet rabbit.**
>
> **The city is beautiful at night.**
>
> **They ran ten kilometres in the race.**

COMPOUND SENTENCES

A compound sentence is one that has two independent clauses joined by a coordinating conjunction.

For example:

Sue sold her pet rabbit, <u>but</u> Preston bought a dog.

John saw a mistake, <u>so</u> he corrected it.

SIMPLE, COMPOUND AND COMPLEX SENTENCES

Look at the compound sentence below which has two independent clauses or sentences and a coordinating conjunction.

Sue bought a pet rabbit, but Preston bought a dog.

  Sue bought a pet rabbit   Preston bought a dog

One independent clause   the other independent clause.

Remember:

A conjunction is a word that joins words, phrases, or clauses.

'But' is a conjunction joining the two independent clauses.

Sue bought a pet rabbit **but** Preston bought a dog.

'But' is referred to as a coordinating conjunction because it coordinates the meanings between the two clauses.

There are several coordinating conjunctions which give different meanings to the sentences of which they are a part. See the next chapter for coordinating conjunctions.

CHAPTER 32

HOW TO USE COORDINATING CONJUNCTIONS

When joining two independent clauses or two simple sentences to make a compound sentence, make sure you are using the correct coordinating conjunction. The coordinating conjunction tells of the relationship between the two sentences that are being joined.

For example:

Relationship between ideas in independent clauses expressed by coordinating conjunctions is as follow.

- When the two ideas are equally important, use 'and'.
- When the two ideas are being contrasted, use 'but', 'yet'.
- When the ideas represent a choice, use 'or'.
- When the ideas represent no choice, use 'nor'.
- When the ideas indicate cause, use 'for'.
- When the ideas indicate effect, use 'so'.

Chapter 33

COMPLEX SENTENCES

A complex sentence is one that has one independent clause and one or more dependent clauses.

For example:

Melissa bought a dress, when she went shopping.

"Melissa bought a dress" is the independent clause.

"when she went shopping" is a dependent clause.

Joining Independent and Dependent or Subordinate clauses

When joining an independent clause and a subordinate clause to make a complex sentence, make sure you are using the correct subordinating conjunction.

An independent clause is a complete sentence.

COMPLEX SENTENCES

A subordinate clause has a subject and a predicate, but it does not express a complete thought as an independent clause does.

Relationship between Clauses using Subordinating Conjunctions is as follow.

- When the subordinate clause expresses cause or reason, use 'because'.
- When the subordinate clause expresses effect or result, use 'so that', 'in order that'.
- When the subordinate clause expresses choice, use 'if', 'whether'.
- When the subordinate clause expresses Contradiction, use 'although', 'even though', 'though'.
- When the subordinate clause expresses place, use 'where', 'wherever'.
- When the subordinate clause expresses time, use 'after,' 'as', 'before', 'once', 'since', 'until', 'when,' 'whenever', 'while'.

CHAPTER 34

SENTENCE ERRORS

There are various types of sentence errors. Here are some of the most common errors: run-on sentence, comma splice, and sentence fragment.

RUN-ON SENTENCES

A common error that many students in high school, college, and university, and even some business people in their online communication, make is the run-on sentence.

Run-on sentences occur when two complete ideas or thoughts are expressed without using proper punctuation to separate the ideas.

For example:

"Sue came home early she was very tired." This is incorrect.

This could be corrected with two sentences:

Sue came home early.

She was very tired.

SENTENCE ERRORS

Or

Sue came home early; she was very tired.

Or

Sue came home early, because she was very tired.

Another example of a run-on sentence is as follows:

"I am going home I will be back soon."

Spoken, these words sound correct, but written, they constitute a run-on sentence.

Another incorrect form of the sentence above is:

"I am going home, I will be back soon." This is also a run-on sentence.

Correct

"I am going home. I will be back soon" or "I am going home; I will be back soon" or "I am going home and will be back soon."

SENTENCE ERRORS

EXPLANATIONS

"I am going home" and "I will be back soon" are two complete ideas, and so can be two separate sentences. When you let two sentences run together without the proper punctuation, it is known as a run-on sentence. A correct form is: I am going home. I will be back soon.

Another explanation in this case is that since the two sentences are so closely related, they can be joined using a semi-colon as in "I am going home; I will be back soon."

EXERCISE

Complete in your notebooks.

Correct the following sentences.

1. Rod went to the store he bought apples.
2. The astronaut prepared for take-off she had been looking forward to this for a long time.
3. Many people believe that they should not work hard they are fooling themselves.
4. The students studied hard all night they were tired the next day.

SENTENCE ERRORS

5. Samantha bought an outfit for graduation it was beautiful.

6. The astronauts arrived at the space station early on Monday they made a space walk the following day.

CHAPTER 35

COMMA SPLICE

A comma splice is when two independent clauses are joined with a comma. This is an error.

For example: (This was used earlier to explain run-on sentences.)

Sue came home early, Sue was very tired.

This could be corrected by making two independent sentences, as shown above in the case of the run-on sentence. For example, "Sue came home early. She was very tired." The sentence could also be corrected by using a semi-colon between the two sentences. For example, it could be corrected this way: "Sue came home early; she was very tired." Another way of correcting the sentence is by joining the two sentences, using a coordinating conjunction. "Sue came home early, because she was very tired."

CHAPTER 36

SENTENCE FRAGMENT

The third type of sentence error mentioned above is the sentence fragment.

As pointed out in our previous chapter, a sentence expresses a complete thought. One of the errors that occur in writing is what is referred to as a sentence fragment.

A sentence fragment is a group of words that does not consist of a complete thought, and so is not a sentence.

In the morning when all the children were at home

Going to the movies

In the sunlight

When you go

Seeing the trees

These examples above are sentence fragments because they need something more to complete the meaning.

SENTENCE FRAGMENT

REVIEW

A sentence expresses a complete thought or idea.

Here are examples of sentences.

Scientists work at the South Pole all year round.

When we travel to South America, we will visit the rain forests.

How to Turn Sentence Fragments into Sentences.

In the morning when all the children were at home, Dad made them a special breakfast.

James and Sue are **going to the movies.**

Plants grow exceedingly well **in the sunlight.**

When you go to university in the fall, will you live on campus?

Seeing the trees, the children knew they were close to the campgrounds.

Remember: The sentence fragments above did not express complete thoughts. They needed something else to express complete thoughts.

SENTENCE FRAGMENT

EXERCISE

In your notebook, complete the following:

Make full sentences from the following sentence fragments.

1. Taking a trip to Scandinavia
2. Going to school in the morning
3. Falling off the ride
4. On the mountains
5. Children shouting at the top of their voices

Note: You can arrange these fragments anywhere in your sentences.

CHAPTER 37

COMMON GRAMMATICAL ERRORS

Correct these sentences. Write in your notebook.

1. John is one of those students who (is, are) always coming in late.
2. One of the students (is, are) coming to the movies with us.
3. Melissa is one of the girls who (want, wants) to become a scientist.
4. One of the people in the office (is, are) the principal of my school.
5. Sam is one of the best players who (have, has) ever played for our team.
6. There (is, are) Mandy and Len.
7. There (go, goes) Sam and Eddie.
8. My friend is one of the dancers who (go, goes) to Europe each year.
9. There (jump, jumps) the athlete.
10. Each of the athletes (play, plays) different positions.

COMMON GRAMMATICAL ERRORS

11. Each student (has, have) a notebook.

12. Each person (get, gets) a prize.

13. The longest day of the year (is, are) in June.

14. The largest of the boxes (contain, contains) the specimen.

CHAPTER 38

ERRORS WITH MODIFIERS

Ambiguous, Dangling and Misplaced Modifiers

The rule is that modifiers must be as close as possible to the words that they modify.

AMBIGUOUS MODIFIER

This is when it is not quite clear what the modifier is modifying.

For example:

We decided <u>in the morning</u> to pack the car and take a long trip.

What is modified by "in the morning?" Is it 'decided' or 'take a long trip'?

The meaning of the sentence could be that **in the morning** we decided to pack the car and take a long trip.

But it could also be that we decided to pack the car and take a long trip **in the morning.**

Dangling Modifier

A dangling modifier is a modifier that dangles some distance from what it modifies.

For example:

I went to the park, having no money. (Incorrect)

'Having no money' does not refer to the 'park,' but to 'I'.

The sentence should read:

"Having no money, I went to the park." (Correct)

The explanation is that it is "I", who was described as "having no money".

Driving through the city, the streets were dirty. (Incorrect)

'Driving through the city' does not refer to 'the streets', but to a subject like 'I'.

The sentences should read:

Driving through the city, I found the streets very dirty. (Correct)

"Driving through the city" cannot refer to "the streets", since it is not the streets that are doing the driving.

MISPLACED MODIFIER

A misplaced modifier is a modifier that is definitely out of place.

For example:

Put the drinks in the refrigerator <u>that is warm</u>. (Incorrect)

'That is warm' is a misplaced modifier, and does not apply to refrigerator, but to 'drinks'.

The sentence could read:

Put the warm drinks in the refrigerator. (Correct)

It is not the refrigerator **that is warm**.

Exercise

In your notebook, think of a few more sentences that you can use to illustrate ambiguous, dangling and misplaced modifiers.

CHAPTER 39

CAPITALIZATION

USE CAPITAL LETTERS FOR THE FOLLOWING CASES:

Proper nouns always begin with capital letters.

Proper nouns include the names of specific people, places, and things. For example, Pope Francis, First Nations, Liberal Party, Mandela, Montreal, New Democratic Party, New York, United Nations, Microsoft, Titanic.

Sentences always begin with a capital letter.

The children read the novels.

When will you go back to Spain?

Several people were invited to the ceremony.

The pronoun "I" is always written with a capital letter.

I have completed my assignments.

When **I** go to the movies, **I** always buy popcorn.

CAPITALIZATION

Personified nouns begin with a capital letter.

People speak of **Father Time**.

Farmers appreciate the goodness of **Mother Earth**.

Capitalize the first letter of days of the week, months, and holidays.

Today is Monday.

The month is April.

We enjoy Christmas holidays.

Capitalize the first letter of titles of books, magazines, newspapers, songs, films, and other writings.

The Life of Martin Luther King

The Toronto Star

What a Wonderful World

Capitalize the names given to a Supreme Being.

God, Jesus Christ, Yahweh, the Almighty, Allah, Buddha

Capitalize the names of sacred texts

Bible, Torah, Koran

Capitalize religions and professions of faith

Christianity, Judaism, Buddhism, Islam, Hinduism

Capitalize the names of languages

English, Spanish, French, Greek, Portuguese, Latin, Sanskrit, Cantonese, Twi, Urdu, Pali, Ojibwa, Oneida.

CHAPTER 40

PUNCTUATION

There are several punctuation marks. The more commonly used ones are period, question mark, comma, semi-colon, colon, exclamation mark, apostrophe, and quotation marks.

PERIOD

Use a period or full stop (.) for the following cases.

A period always comes at the end of a sentence.

For example:

I will go to school tomorrow.

A period comes after a command that is given without emphasis.

For example:

Please help me.

A period comes after abbreviations and initials

For example:

Mr. B. S. Jones

Question Mark

Use a question mark (?) in the following cases.

A question mark comes at the end of a question.

For example:

Where are you going?

A question mark comes at the end of a word that asks a question.

For example:

Who? What?

Comma

Use a comma (,) in the following situations:

A comma comes between parts of an address, the date, or a title.

For example:

255 St. Jean Street, Montreal, Canada H3Y 2Y4.

June 17, 2000.

A comma comes after the greeting in an informal letter.

For example:

Dear Susie,   Dear Patrick,

A comma comes between words and phrases that make up a series.

For example:

The important parts of an essay are the introduction, body, and conclusion.

A comma is used to separate parts of a sentence that are not essential.

For example:

The children, who live in the neighbourhood, came to our play.

A comma is used after an introductory element in a sentence.

For example:

In conclusion, they found a solution to the problem.

A comma should come before a coordinating conjunction that joins independent clauses.

For example:

The boys went to the rural areas. The girls went to the cities.

The new sentence should read:

"The boys went to the rural areas**,** **and** the girls went to the cities."

CHAPTER 41

MORE ABOUT PUNCTUATION

SEMI-COLON

A semicolon (;) is used to join parts of a compound sentence when they are not joined by a conjunction.

For example:

There are many people in the house; we must leave now.

A semicolon comes before words such as therefore, however, and nevertheless, to connect two independent clauses.

For example:

We went to the city; however, we left early enough to return to the game.

A semicolon comes before explanatory expressions.

For example:

There are several reasons why people come to this location; namely, convenience, cost, and fashion.

Colon

A colon (:) is used after a statement that is followed by a list.

For example:

The children brought many things: books, pencils, crayons, and pens.

A colon is used after the greeting in a business letter.

For example:

Dear Mr. Jones:

A colon is used to separate hours from minutes.

For example:

5:15 a.m., 4:40 p.m.

Exclamation Mark

An exclamation mark (!) is used after a word, phrase, or sentence to show that it was said in surprise or suddenly.

For example:

Help! Wow!

Apostrophe

An apostrophe (') is also used to show possession or to indicate when something has been omitted.

Apostrophe is used to show possession.

When you want to say something belongs to someone, an apostrophe is used.

For example:

This book belongs to John - This is John's book.

MORE ABOUT PUNCTUATION

An apostrophe is used to show that something is omitted.

For example:

"Do not" can be written as **"don't"**.

"It is" can be written as **it's.**

QUOTATION MARKS

Use quotation marks (" ") in the following cases.

Quotation marks go around the direct words of a speaker.

For example:

He said: "Tell me an interesting story."

Quotation marks go around the titles of songs and poems.

For example:

"Happy Birthday to You," and "Ode to a Grecian Urn."

CHAPTER 42

PARALLEL STRUCTURE

When writing words, phrases, or clauses in a series, you must ensure that they have the same grammatical structure.

For example:

Lena is kind, considerate, and helps a great deal. (Faulty structure)

Lena is kind, considerate and helpful. (Correct)

Talking and to laugh are fun. (Faulty structure)

Talking and laughing are fun. (Correct)

The students went to school, studied their English, and were doing their exam. (Faulty structure)

The students went to school, studied their English, and did their exam. (Correct)

CHAPTER 43

WHO AND WHOM

'Who' is the subject and 'whom' is the object.

WHEN TO USE "WHO"

I saw the boy. **The boy** worked late. (Subject)

I saw the boy **who** worked late. (Subject)

When joining the sentences, use **who** since the word that you are replacing is the **subject** in its sentence. You are replacing **'the boy"** which is the subject of the second sentence. Therefore, you must use **'who'**.

WHEN TO USE 'WHOM'

I saw the boy. I recommended **the boy**. (Object)

I saw the boy whom I recommended. (Object)

When joining these sentences, you want to replace 'the boy' with either who or whom. You want to replace 'the boy' in the second sentence. But **"the boy"** in the second sentence is the object of that sentence. Therefore, you must use "whom".

There is another occasion when you must use "whom" and not "who".

For example:

Give the book to the teacher.

If you did not know who should receive the book, you may ask,

"To **whom** should I give the book?

In this situation, when the word 'to' has to be used, you must use **"whom"**, since **'to'** always takes the object.

EXERCISE

In your notebook, join these sentences using "who" or whom".

1. I saw John. John is my friend.
2. The teacher introduced me to the principal. The principal recently came to the school.
3. Harry gave the picture to his wife. I find his wife is very friendly.
4. I visited Pat. They took Pat to the hospital last night.

CHAPTER 44

CONTRACTIONS

Use contractions when combining a verb with a negative and when combining a subject pronoun with a verb.

Contractions are formed from a verb with a negative

Aren't	Are not
Can't	Cannot
Couldn't	Could not
Didn't	Did not
Doesn't	Does not
Don't	Do not
Hadn't	Had not
Hasn't	Has not
Haven't	Have not
Isn't	Is not
Mightn't	Might not
Mustn't	Must not

CONTRACTIONS

Shouldn't	Should not
Wasn't	Was not
Weren't	Were not
Won't	Will not

Contractions are formed from a Subject Pronoun with a Verb

He'd	He would
He'll	He will
He's	He is
I'd	I would
I'll	I will
I'm	I am
It's	It is
I've	I have
She'd	She would
She'll	She will
She's	She is
They'd	They would
They'll	They will
They're	They are

CONTRACTIONS

They've	They have
We'd	We would
We'll	We will
We're	We are
We've	We have
You'd	You would
You'll	You will
You're	You are
You've	You have

Never make contractions with noun and verb.

For example:

Never say "Sue's going home." (Incorrect)

Say "Sue is going home." (Correct)

For example:

Never say "John's coming to the movies with me."

Say "John is coming to the movies with me.".

CONTRACTIONS

Note:

Never say "The dog is wagging it's tail." (Incorrect)

It's in this case means **it is**.

Say "The dog is wagging its tail." (Correct)

CHAPTER 45

SHORT REVIEW

It is rather commonplace to see the following sentences:

You're sister is here.

Your going home.

Your invited to a seminar.

Its warm inside.

It's tail is short.

These are all wrong. When speaking, these errors are not apparent, but when written, they stand out.

Corrections to the Incorrect Sentences Above

Incorrect : "You're sister is here."

Correct: "Your sister is here."

Explanation: "You're" – means "You are"

 "Your" is a possessive adjective describing the noun 'sister'.

Incorrect : "Your going home."

Correct: "You are going home" or "You're going home."

SHORT REVIEW

Incorrect: "Your invited to a seminar"

Correct: "You are invited to a seminar" or "You're invited to a seminar."

Incorrect: "Its warm inside."

Correct: "It's warm inside" or "It is warm inside."

Explanation: it's stands for "it is"

Incorrect : "It's tail is short."

Correct: "Its tail is short".

Explanation: "Its" is a possessive adjective describing "tail".

CHAPTER 46

VOCABULARY BUILDING

INCREASE YOUR VOCABULARY AND IMPROVE YOUR SPELLING.

Make your personal dictionary.

WORDS FREQUENTLY MISUSED

KNOW THE DIFFERENCE IN MEANING AND USE OF THESE WORDS IN SENTENCES.

Affect	Effect		
Bear	Bare	Beer	Bier
Among	Between		
Accent	Ascent		
Board	Bored		
Capital	Capitol		
Cereal	Serial		
Corporation	Cooperation		

VOCABULARY BUILDING

Decent	Descent		
Dear	Deer		
Desert	Dessert		
Diner	Dinner		
Good	Well		
Here	Hear	Hare	Hair
Hour	Our		
How	Who		
Human	Humane		
Knight	Night		
Later	Latter	Letter	
Lose	Loose		
Once	Ounce		
Patience	Patients		
Real	Really		
Respectfully	Respectively		
Role	Roll		
Super	Supper		
Tale	Tail		
Their	There		

VOCABULARY BUILDING

Two	Too	To
Union	Onion	
Wear	Were	Where

MY PERSONAL DICTIONARY AND WORKSHEETS

CHAPTER 47

STRETCHING MY VOCABULARY

WORDS FREQUENTLY MISSPELLED

EXERCISE

In your notebook, write out these words and make sentences with each. DO NOT GUESS. Use your dictionary, when necessary.

This activity will not only help you remember the words and their meanings, but will also ensure you know how to use them in sentences.

Abrupt	Adapt	Adept	Adopt	
Advertise	Advice	Advise	Annual	
Apartment	Appearance	Arctic	Arrange	
Article	Associate	Aspirate	Aspire	
Asthma	Assignment	Athlete	Athletic	Aviator
Bouquet	Banquet			
Column				
Diarrhea	Dictionary	Diphtheria		

STRETCHING MY VOCABULARY

Disappoint   Dying   Dyeing

Ecstasy   Exasperate   Exaggerate

Eligible   Environment

Fiancé   Fiancée   Finance   Forty-Four

Khaki   Knee   Knelt

Mantel   Mantle   Misspell

Necessary   Ninety

Occasion   Occurred

Particular   Picnic   Practical   Practice

Practise   Precede   Principal   Principle

Privilege   Proceed   Procedure

Prophecy   Prophesy   Psalm   Pursue

Reactivate   Resuscitate   Rhythm

Schedule   Separate   Serial   Similar

Surprise

Useable   Usual   Unusual

Vaccine   Validate   Vaccinate

Valediction

MY PERSONAL DICTIONARY AND WORKSHEETS

Chapter 48

SPELLING CHALLENGE

EXERCISE

One of the two words on each line is incorrect. Write the correct word in your notebook. Check all words in your dictionary to make sure you know which is the correct spelling. **DO NOT GUESS.**

Appearance	Apperance
Arangement	Arrangement
Assignment	Asingment
Embarrassment	Embarasment
Enviroment	Environment
Government	Goverment
Harassment	Harrassment
Hiccough	Hicough
Hickcups	Hiccups
Imply	Implie
Improvment	Improvement

SPELLING CHALLENGE

Independent   Independant

Infer   Infir

Invesstigate   Investigate

Recommendation   Reccomendation

Refrigerator   Refridgerator

Superintendent   Suprintendant

MY SPELLING CHALLENGE WORDS

CHAPTER 49

SINGLE WORDS USED FOR PHRASES

Phrase	Word
A number of bees living together	hive
A number of lions living together in the wild	pride
A number of seals, sea lions or penguins living together	rookery
A number of cattle living together	herd
A number of birds moving together	flight
A number of ants living together	nest
A number of horses harnessed together	team
A number of dogs, cats, or pigs born at the same time	litter
A collection of domesticated birds, such as chickens, ducks, and turkeys	poultry
A collection of people at a football game	spectators
A collection of people in church	congregation
A collection of people in the street	crowd
A collection of dancers	troupe
A collection of people who sing in a church	choir

SINGLE WORDS USED FOR PHRASES

A collection of soldiers	army, troop
A collection of sailors operating a ship	crew
A collection of judges or bishops	bench
A collection of poems	anthology
A collection of flowers	bouquet
A collection of ships	fleet

CHAPTER 50

SINGLE WORDS INDICATING PLACES

Phrase	Phrase
A place where beehives of honey bees are kept	apiary
A place where birds are kept	aviary
A place where fishes are kept	aquarium
A place where horses are kept	stable
A place where dogs are kept	kennel
A place where lions are born when in the wild	den
A place where lions live in captivity	zoo
A place where medicines are dispensed	dispensary, pharmacy
A place where monks or priests live	monastery
A place where nuns live	convent
A place where beer is produced	brewery
A place where airplanes are housed	hangar
A place where books are kept	library
A place where old government documents are kept	archives

SINGLE WORDS USED FOR PHRASES

A place where scientific experiments are conducted — laboratory

A place where art treasures are kept — museum

A place where astronomical observations are made — observatory

A place where water is collected and held for an area — reservoir

A place where plants are started and grown toa certain age before being planted in the garden — nursery

A place for new born babies in the hospital — nursery

NEXT SECTION - BRINGING IT ALL TOGETHER

The reason that we try to improve our writing, grammar, and spelling skills is so that we are able to improve our comprehension. Now that we have gone through some of the more common errors above, let us try out some comprehension skills.

CHAPTER 51

INVENTION OF A POPULAR SPORT: BASKETBALL

1892. It was a brutally cold winter, and Luther Gulick, the head of the Physical Education Department at the School of Christian Workers in Springfield, Massachusetts, was somewhat perplexed. He asked his staff to help create an "athletic distraction" for the young men in their classes. The challenge was to create a game that could be played indoors, when it was just too cold for the young men to play outside.

One of these physical education instructors who took up this challenge was 30-year old James Naismith. Naismith struggled to create an energetic and exciting game that would hold the young men's interest. When it appeared that he could not meet the deadline, he considered the possibility of introducing lacrosse and soccer to be played in the gym. He soon realized, though, that these two games were too physical to be accommodated indoors.

INVENTION OF A POPULAR SPORT: BASKETBALL

Naismith almost gave up, and then he had a bright idea. Why not introduce the game, duck-on-a-rock, that he played as a young boy outside the one-room schoolroom he attended? He used some of the principles and created a new game. He nailed a half-bushel peach basket to the opposite ends of the balcony around the gym.

The staff and students at the school tried out their first game on March 11, 1892. They were very pleased with the results as they found the game quite engaging. They wanted to call it Naismith Ball, but Naismith, being the humble man that he was, called the game Basket Ball. This appeared a fitting name for the game, considering that it was played with a basket and a soccer ball. Naismith developed a set of 13 rules to be used with the game, twelve of which are still basic to the game today. It took a decade for the bottoms of the peach baskets to be removed, so the ball did not have to be retrieved manually after every shot. The game first spread in Canada, which was also quite fitting, since Naismith was a Canadian.

Early Life

Born in Almonte, a small town 30 miles south of Ottawa in Ontario, on November 6, 1861, Naismith was orphaned when he was only 9, and his education suffered as a result. Ian Naismith, grandson of James Naismith, reported that "[a] relative rescued James, along with his sister and brother, by sleigh. The three orphans were raised by an uncle and other relatives." Until his death on March 21, 2012, Ian Naismith was to honour his grandfather's memory by being the founder and director of the International Basketball Foundation, an organization that promoted youth sports.

According to reports, when James Naismith was 10, he went to work in lumber camps and on farms in the area to help out the family. He dropped out of school at 15, thinking that there was no good reason for him to continue. At that time, he had found a permanent job as a lumberjack. He would have continued working at this job, had something unusual not happened.

INVENTION OF A POPULAR SPORT: BASKETBALL

As Ian Naismith reported, "[a]t the age of 19, he (James Naismith) walked into a local bar and ordered a whiskey. A man standing next to him, cap pulled low over his eyes, spoke to James without turning his head." The younger Naismith then quoted the conversation that ensued between the man and James.

"Ye're Margaret Young's son, aren't ye?"

"Aye," James replied, reaching for his drink.

"She'd turn over in her grave to see ye."

Ian Naismith reported that according to his grandfather, this was a major turning point in his grandfather's life. "James set the whiskey down – never to drink again. That night, he made a silent vow to his dead mother that she would never again be ashamed of him."

JAMES NAISMITH WENT BACK TO SCHOOL

James Naismith changed his life that night, and decided to go back to school. After dropping out of school in 1877 with only two years of high school, he went back in 1881 at the age of 20, and graduated in 1883.

He later attended McGill University in Montreal, Canada, where he played a variety of sports, including football, lacrosse, rugby, golf and fencing. He was an outstanding athlete, and received the Silver Wickstead Medal as the all-round athlete at McGill in 1885. In 1887, he received the Gold Wickstead Medal, and graduated with a philosophy degree that very year. Naismith considered becoming a minister, and so studied religion, working towards another degree. He won the Silver Medal for his work in theology at Presbyterian College in 1890.

However, an incident during one of his games caused him to change his career path from that of becoming a minister to that of becoming a physical education instructor. While Naismith was with teammates, very possibly after a game, one of them used an obscene word. On realizing that Naismith was around and heard him, his teammate apologized to Naismith for his poor conduct. This simple incident convinced Naismith that he might just be able to help people to improve their lives through sports as through the ministry.

Therefore, on graduating in 1890 with a degree in religion, Naismith joined the Department of Christian Workers as an instructor, and it was while in this capacity that he invented the game of Basket Ball, as he called it.

BASKET BALL WENT INTERNATIONAL

The game grew in popularity. Probably because Naismith was a Canadian, Canadians took a special interest in the game. One of the five Canadians who had played the original game back on March 11, 1892, was Lyman Archibald, who introduced the game to the YMCA in St. Stephens, New Brunswick, that very year. The game was also played in Montreal in 1892. When Archibald moved to Hamilton, Ontario, in 1893, he also introduced the game there. That same year, the game was played at the University of Toronto and a year later at McGill University in Montreal, where a basket ball trophy was offered for the competition between faculty and students.

The game also grew in popularity in the United States, but within five years it was prohibited in some places, because of the competitive nature of the sport that often led to serious conflicts between opposing teams. Also, in the United States, small groups of basket ball players would often take over a YMCA gym, making it difficult for other athletes to have a chance to participate in their own sports. In time, the YMCA members who were prohibited from playing basket ball in a YMCA gymnasium terminated their membership and rented other halls in which to play the game.

In the 1890s, the game was introduced to France, England, Brazil, Australia, China, India and Japan, and by 1901, it was played in Iran.

NAISMITH CONTINUED HIS CAREER AND STUDIES

Despite the popularity of the game, Naismith did not seek publicity for his accomplishment. Between 1890 and 1895, he served as a physical education instructor, first in the Department of Christian Workers at the YMCA Training School, which became known later as Springfield College. Naismith served in the same capacity at the Denver YMCA from 1895 to 1898. In 1898, he earned a medical degree from Gross Medical School at the University of Colorado. Naismith then became assistant professor and chapel director at the University of Kansas from 1898 to 1909, and served as professor and university physician at the same institution from 1909 to 1917.

However, he had an interruption in his positions as professor and university physician during the First World War. Naismith served as Chaplain and Captain in the First Kansas Infantry between 1914 and 1917, actually serving as part of the infantry on the Mexican Border in 1916. Naismith also served as YMCA Secretary for 19 months in France and 3 months in the United States between 1917 and 1919.

Naismith was ordained a Presbyterian minister and served as a physical education professor until 1937. In 1939, Naismith received a Doctor of Divinity Degree from McGill University.

BASKETBALL'S POPULARITY

The game of basketball became quite popular over the years and it was introduced as a sport at the Olympic Games held in Berlin in 1936. By that time, the game was called basketball, and had become a well-organized sport. The National Association of Basketball Coaches sponsored Naismith to go to Berlin to see the introduction of the game as an Olympic sport. Three years after this event, and the very year Naismith graduated with a Doctors of Divinity Degree from McGill, he died. Naismith wrote extensively about athletics and is credited with inventing the football helmet.

He could never have imagined the great strides his game would have made in the future, and of the prominent sport that basketball is the world over.

NAISMITH'S RECOGNITION

The Naismith Basketball Hall of Fame was organized as an honorary society on November 28, 1939. In 1959, Naismith was inducted into the Basketball Hall of Fame. In

1968, the first location of the Basketball Hall of Fame was established at Springfield College, and in 1985, the Hall of Fame was relocated to downtown Springfield. On September 28, 2002, the Basketball Hall of Fame paid tribute to Naismith by developing a New Hall of Fame, which is still in Springfield, but is now a three-storey spherical museum, with 35,000 square feet of exhibit space, three theatres, interactive kiosks where basketball fans could test their knowledge of basketball memorabilia, and a McDonald's Basketball-themed restaurant, a Reebok Concept Store, and the Hall of Fame gift shop.

Naismith's Memorial Basketball Hall of Fame was created and Naismith's name is emblazoned there in recognition for his ingenuity in creating the game of basketball. The game continues to hold the interest of millions of players all around the world. According to the Basketball Hall of Fame, basketball is a sport that over 300 million people in more than 200 countries play. The mission of the Hall of Fame is to continue to promote the game.

COMPREHENSION QUESTIONS

1. Close to what major Canadian city was James Naismith born?

2. At what age did he return to high school after dropping out?

3. Why was this the case?

4. What incident caused Naismith to stop drinking and return to high school?

5. What sport did Naismith play when he was at McGill University?

6. Why did Naismith not become a minister?

7. How did he come to invent basketball? What were the circumstances?

8. How did the climate play a role in the invention of basketball?

9. On what occasion was Naismith recognized as being the inventor of basketball?

10. How popular is the sport of basketball?

11. Who is James Naismith's grandson? What did he do?

INVENTION OF A POPULAR SPORT: BASKETBALL

12. What do you know about the Naismith Basketball Hall of Fame?

13. If you play basketball, why do you?

14. What do you find interesting about basketball?

15. Who is your favourite basketball player?

16. Have you ever visited the Naismith Basketball Hall of Fame?

RESEARCH POSSIBILITIES

1. Discuss the sport of basketball in a country other than Canada or the United States.

2. Discuss the involvement of women in the sport of basketball.

3. Write a biography of your favourite basketball player.

Chapter 52

I DO AND I UNDERSTAND

Now that you are at the end of this book, I hope you have done all the exercises recommended. If you have not, you can still go back and complete them. These exercises were intended to help you understand some of the concepts that you may not have known or that you may have forgotten.

Confucius is quoted as saying, "I hear and I forget. I see and I remember. I do and I understand." Take his counsel and do the exercises. You will surely understand them better.

MORE READING AVAILABLE

If you found this book beneficial, you may also want to consider trying out some of the other books in this series. See the back of the book for details. You may also want to send us comments at info@IsraelinShockness.com

"Thanks for reading! If you found this book useful, please post a short review where you obtained this book. I read all the reviews personally so I can get your feedback and make this book even better.

www.ingramcontent.com/pod-product-compliance
Lightning Source LLC
Chambersburg PA
CBHW060523100426
42743CB00009B/1418